DATE LOANED

A Children's Museum
Activity Book

MILK CARTON BLOCKS

A Children's Museum Activity Book

MILK CARTON BLOCKS

by Bernie Zubrowski

Illustrated by Otto Coontz

Little, Brown and Company
Boston   Toronto

Children's Museum Activity Books in This Series

BUBBLES

BALL-POINT PENS

MILK CARTON BLOCKS

Library of Congress Cataloging in Publication Data

Zubrowski, Bernie.

   A Children's Museum activity book: Milk carton blocks.
   SUMMARY: Directions for making three sizes of building blocks from milk cartons and for building structures commonly found in houses and buildings, including towers, furniture, and arches.
   1. Paperwork—Juvenile literature. 2. Cartons—Juvenile literature. 3. Milk—Containers—Juvenile literature. [1. Paperwork. 2. Handicraft. 3. Building] I. Coontz, Otto. II. Title. III. Title: Milk carton building blocks. IV. Series: Boston. Children's Museum. A Children's Museum activity book.
TT870.Z8   793.4   78-27215
ISBN 0-316-98884-7
ISBN 0-316-98885-5 pbk.

Published simultaneously in Canada
by Little, Brown & Company (Canada) Limited
PRINTED IN THE UNITED STATES OF AMERICA

A Children's Museum
Activity Book

MILK CARTON BLOCKS

INTRODUCTION

The use of bricks to build houses and other kinds of structures started five or six thousand years ago. Before that, mud or clay was used to make the walls of houses. It was in the ancient kingdom of Mesopotamia that mud and clay were made into regular shapes and dried in the sun. Eventually, it was discovered that firing clay would result in a more permanent material, and bricks began to be widely used.

The way bricks are piled up to make walls can make a great deal of difference in how strong the walls are. You have probably discovered this concept while playing with wooden blocks. Using small blocks can give you some feeling for this balance. But working with larger blocks is more exciting and will also show you better how to balance the forces in the wall so that it stands up.

If you're going to use this book, you'll need blocks. Where do you get them? It would take a lot of time and money to build a set of large wooden blocks. There are other materials that can be used, however. Half-gallon milk cartons or shoe boxes make very good substitutes. With the help of your friends in your neighborhood or in your school, you can collect hundreds in a few weeks. It may take awhile to get enough for a major project, but even with a few blocks you can experiment with small structures.

PUTTING TOGETHER
A SET OF BLOCKS

The empty milk cartons themselves might be used as blocks. However, for two reasons you will soon find that they are not that satisfactory. First, one end is not square. Second, walls made with empty milk cartons tip over easily.

Here is how to make a block that has two square ends and enough weight so that walls made with it will not tip over easily.

YOU WILL NEED:

Newspaper
Masking tape
Lots of sand
A can about standard soup size
As many milk cartons as you can get, well rinsed

Most bricks are half as wide as they are long.
The present design of a half-gallon milk carton
is such that you can make three sizes of blocks.
The first size will be just long enough to cover
the width of two blocks just below it.

TO MAKE A BLOCK:

1. Open a carton as shown in the picture.
2. Empty two full cans of sand on four sheets of newspaper.
3. Fold the newspaper so that no sand can come out.

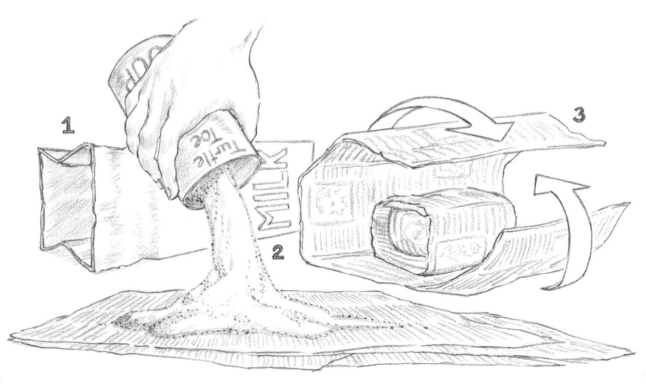

4. Put these packets of sand into one carton with flaps fully opened. Tape or staple the flaps flat.

5. Cut off the folded end of another carton.

6. Slide this on top of the carton filled with sand, squeezing the sides of the bottom carton as shown.

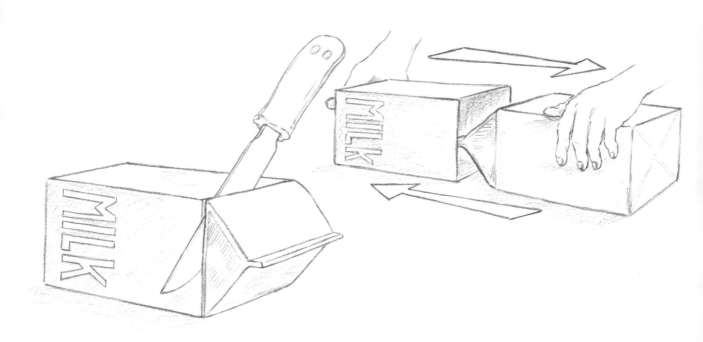

7. If you want to be doubly sure no sand will come out, wind another piece of tape around the crack where the two cartons join.

TO MAKE A HALF-SIZE BLOCK:

1. Cut one milk carton as shown.

CUT TOP ⇨

3 INCHES

CUT HALF WAY DOWN EACH SIDE

2. Put sand rolled up in newspaper as shown on page 12.

3. Cut another milk carton in half.

CUT HERE

3 INCHES = ONE HALF

4. Fold the cut flaps of the first carton—
one flap on top of another.

5. Squeeze the bottom of the carton from
step 3 onto this one.

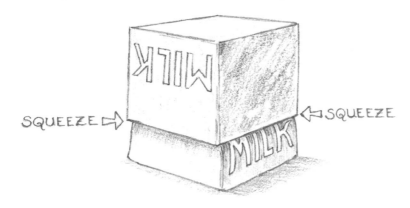

TO MAKE A TRIANGULAR BLOCK:

Cut one milk carton in the following way.

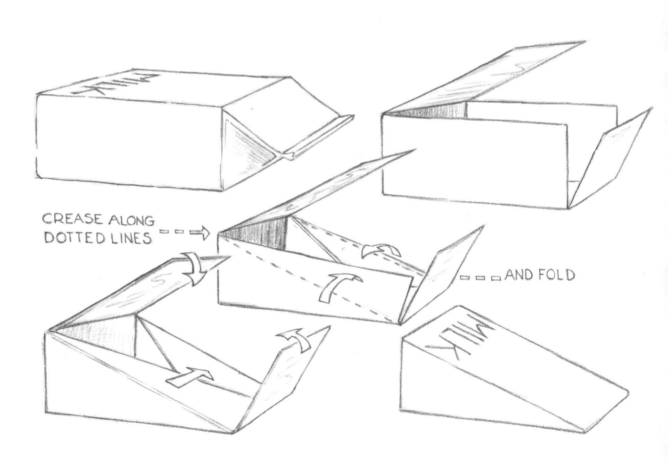

CREASE ALONG
DOTTED LINES ◖ ◖ ➤

◖ ◖ ◖ AND FOLD

Triangular blocks will be useful in making arches or roofs.

Forming an assembly line will help put many blocks together quickly.

Try to find a room in the house, such as a basement or attic, where you can store and play with your blocks without making a mess.

When you have a hundred or more blocks, you are ready to make houses, towers, bridges, arches, tunnels, and even furniture.

TOWERS

How tall a tower can you make with the blocks
you have made? What is the tallest tower you
can make with twenty-five blocks?

In building towers you may have found that placing the blocks a certain way made a steadier tower. Here are some experiments to try to help you think about the way bricks are stacked.

Which way of stacking will give you a taller tower standing by itself?

STACKED OVERLAPPING

STACKED ON ENDS

STACKED ON SIDES

STACKED IN ROWS

Suppose paper were placed like mortar between the blocks. Would this make a steadier tower? Try placing masking tape along the cracks. Does this strengthen your tower?

Having experimented with ways of stacking,
how high can you make a tower now?

Chimneys

Short chimneys are usually square in shape.

Smokestacks for factories are usually circular and very tall.

Have you ever seen very tall smokestacks that are square in shape? Is there any advantage in having a circular instead of a square one?

Columns—An experiment

Columns are related to smokestacks in their shape. However, while smokestacks are free standing, columns are used to hold up other weights in a building, such as the roof or an upper floor. While they hold up the building, it pushes down on them tightly and keeps them from tipping over.

Here is an experiment to try. Which shape of a paper column—triangular, square, or circular—will support the most weight?

1. Cut an 8½″ × 11″ piece of paper in half.

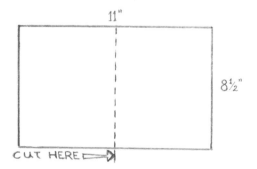

2. Next, mark off a quarter-inch-wide strip.

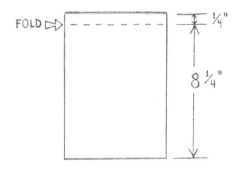

3. To make a triangular column, fold the remaining 8¼″ into three equal spaces.

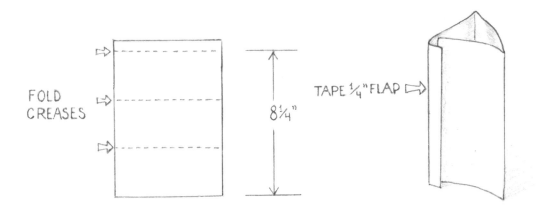

4. Mark off a quarter-inch strip on the second half of the paper, and divide the remaining area into four equal spaces to get a square column.

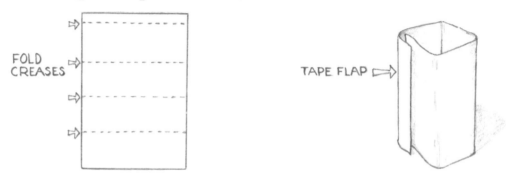

FOLD CREASES

TAPE FLAP

5. You can test each column by placing a can on top of it, and adding weight to the can till the column tips over. Sand or nails are weights you could use.

NAILS

SAND

SODA

Count the nails as you gently drop them into the can. If you are using sand, it may take more than one full can to bend the column. Try to catch the can when the column begins to bend.

Do this again to see if you get approximately the same results. How does the amount needed to break the triangular column compare to that used to break the square column?

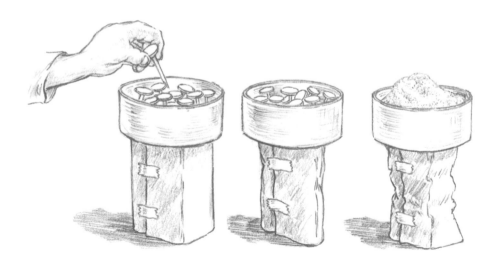

Make a circular column by bending a half sheet of paper into a circle and letting one end overlap a quarter inch.

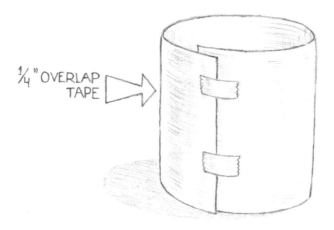

¼" OVERLAP
TAPE

How does the support of the circular column compare to that of the other shapes?

Try making columns of different heights. Before testing them with weights, can you guess whether a tall column will be stronger or weaker than a short one?

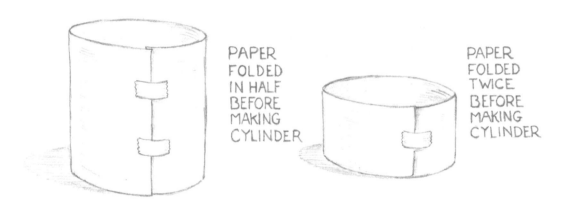

PAPER FOLDED IN HALF BEFORE MAKING CYLINDER

PAPER FOLDED TWICE BEFORE MAKING CYLINDER

You can also see how much sand or nails one, two, three, or four cylinders will hold.

HOUSES

Milk-carton building blocks are big, and if you had enough of them you could build a big house. With enough blocks you and some friends could build a house that you could walk into.

Just because the blocks are rectangular doesn't mean you have to build a rectangular house. Design your own house, with rooms of all shapes.

Looking closely at walls

When building houses with the blocks, you probably noticed that sometimes walls are steady, and sometimes they tip over easily. Does the way the blocks are piled up make much difference in whether the wall will tip over easily, or not?

It might be useful for you to look closely at a brick wall or a brick house. Take a walk around your neighborhood. Look at how bricks are put together to make a wall or house.

The drawings on this page show several kinds of walls. Which do you think will stand up under a strong wind? Which do you think will tip over with just a little push?

Try making these same walls with your blocks. See if you can design other kinds of strong walls with the blocks.

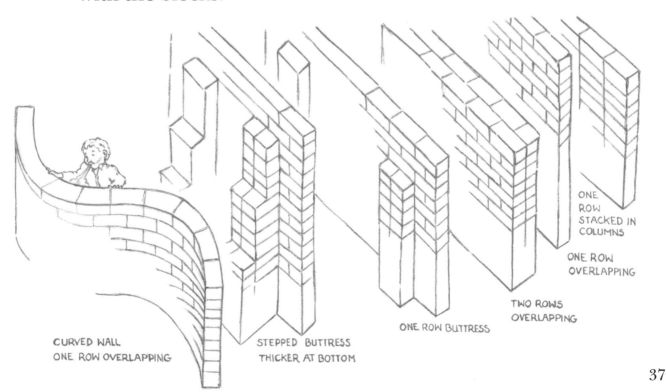

CURVED WALL
ONE ROW OVERLAPPING

STEPPED BUTTRESS
THICKER AT BOTTOM

ONE ROW BUTTRESS

TWO ROWS
OVERLAPPING

ONE ROW OVERLAPPING

ONE ROW STACKED IN COLUMNS

Foundations

In building real houses and walls, a hole is dug in the ground first. Cement is poured and allowed to become hard. This foundation is thicker than the wall above it. The purpose of the foundation is to prevent the wall or house from sinking into the ground.

More support for your house

Another way of giving support to your house is by making a stick structure first. You can construct this framework out of broomsticks, or dowels, which most lumberyards sell. Use large rubber bands to hold the sticks together.

FURNITURE

Once you have built your house, you might want to have some chairs or tables inside and outside the house. If your blocks have been made solid enough, they can be used to sit on.

Can you make contoured chairs similar to arches?

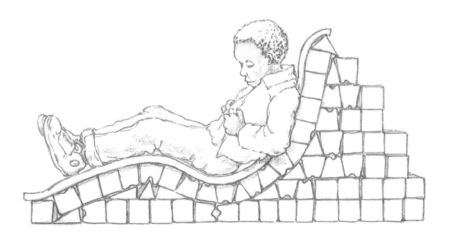

BEAMS

If you want windows in your house, you will need some sort of beam to span the width of the window. A piece of wood could be used. The real challenge is to stay with the materials you have right with you and make some sort of beam.

Here is one way of making a beam using milk cartons.

1. Fold two milk cartons into hollow blocks.
2. Cut off both ends of an empty milk carton as shown in the diagram.

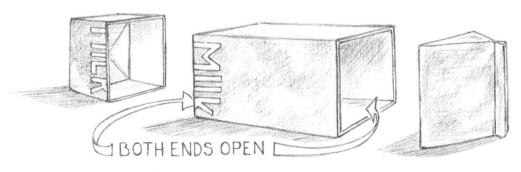

BOTH ENDS OPEN

3. Stuff a block into each end of the hollow carton.

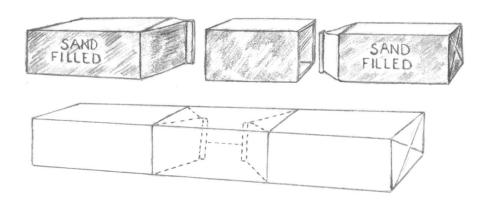

If your beam needs to be longer, repeat the above steps.

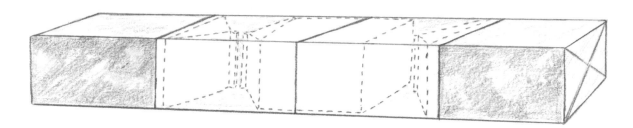

Experimenting with beams

Using milk cartons and other kinds of materials, what is the largest distance you can span with each?

WITH MILK CARTONS

How long a beam can you put together before it begins to sag when placed between two tables?

WITH DRINKING STRAWS

To make two straws into one long straw you can put them together in the following manner:

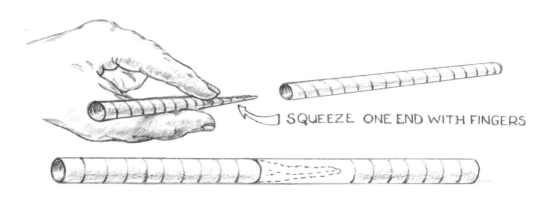

SQUEEZE ONE END WITH FINGERS

How many straws can you add to each other before the beam falls to the floor?

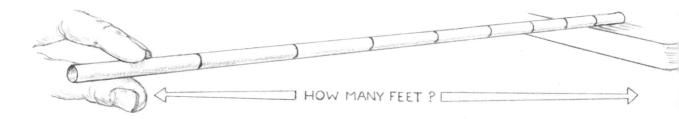

HOW MANY FEET?

WITH PAPER

Cut an 8½″ × 11″ sheet of paper into sections. Make a triangular, square, or circular column as shown on the preceding pages.

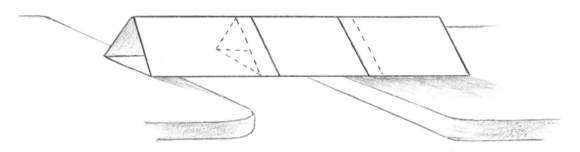

How much weight can a beam hold before it breaks? You could use sand or nails in an empty cardboard frozen juice can.

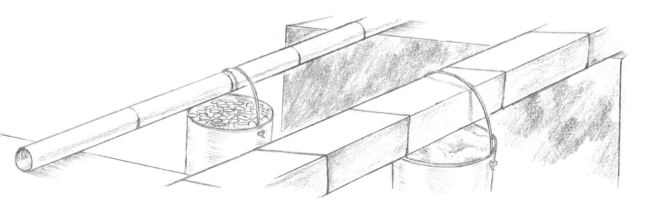

Putting the beams to work

Now that you know how to put beams together, the possibilities for even more structures with different shapes appear. Making tunnels is one idea. Can you make up some of your own?

BRIDGES

Some of the earliest bridges were just stones laid across streams. Other kinds of simple bridges were piles of rock or brick with planks of wood spanning the distances between the piles.

Using blocks, or even beams, try building various kinds of bridges. See how wide a gap you can span between two piles of blocks using wooden planks, or using beams made from milk cartons. In building these bridges, be careful to make them close to the floor; when you test them and they start to tip, you don't want to fall very far.

CORBELS AND ARCHES

A beam is one simple way of spanning spaces with blocks. In the past people have used other ways of arranging blocks to make doorways or open spaces in walls.

In ancient Mesopotamia and Egypt, layers of stone or brick were stacked as shown below.

Each row of bricks overhangs the one below. A row of bricks that hangs out over a lower row to create an open space within a wall is a kind of *corbel*. This structure is one arrangement builders have developed for holding up roofs or upper stories of houses. Can you make a corbel with your blocks?

How wide a doorway can you make with this kind of construction?

If you have trouble keeping the walls from falling, go back to the section on houses and refresh your memory.

The *arch* is another structure that will hold up walls without having to be supported from below. The Romans used the arch in building bridges and aqueducts that stretched for many miles. Some of these constructions are still standing today.

Of wood and stone

If you look around in your neighborhood, you may find several examples of arches. Also, when you are traveling around in the city, count how many times the arch has been used in building entrances, as an opening for windows, or as a bridge spanning a river or a highway.

Of blocks

Arches are made from blocks of a special shape. You will need to bend the milk carton blocks to imitate this shape.

Since the sides of the cartons are very smooth, the blocks tend to slide when placed on top of each other. You can prevent this by gluing sandpaper to the sides or by gluing the blocks together.

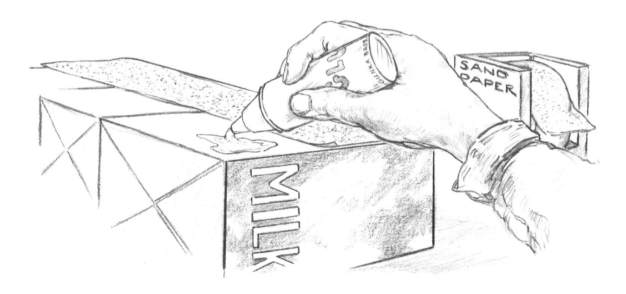

With a broomstick, press down on the long side of the block.

Press until it looks like this.

The boys in the following pictures did not use glue to hold the blocks together. They just used the force of the blocks pushing against each other to hold the arch up.

To hold the blocks while they were stacking them, they used the box.

Why have blocks been put on top and on the sides of the arch?

How long a tunnel can you make with a row of arches?

After you have built an arch, here are some questions to consider.

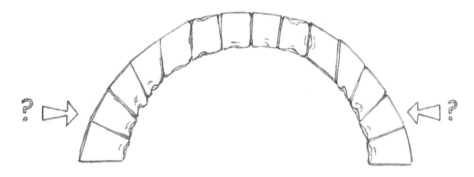

How many blocks can you put on top of the arch before it will fall?

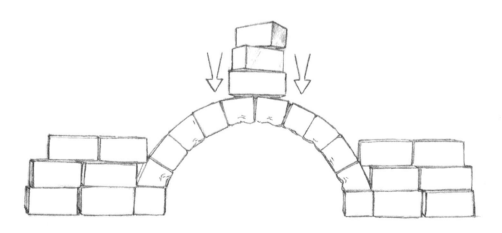

What is the widest gap that you can span with an arch?

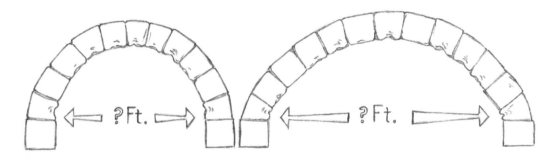

Another kind of arch is used in doorways of buildings. Can you make one like the following using the regular and the slanted blocks?

CONCLUSION

Most of the structures shown in this book are commonly found in houses and buildings. There are still other ways of stacking blocks or arranging them into patterns. By looking at books on architecture or ones showing houses of other cultures, you will find even more ideas for projects you can do with your blocks.

Try inventing new shapes of blocks, and see what kinds of houses you can build with these. See if you can design differently shaped walls or rooftops that not only are strong but also look nice. In fact, some people feel that houses can be like giant sculptures. See what interesting sculptures you can make by stacking the blocks into unusual shapes. Whatever you do, keep your blocks around so that you can continually experiment in making new structures.